Universal Laws:
The Comprehensive
Study Guide

by

Jeremy Lopez

ENDORSEMENTS

You are put on this earth with incredible potential and a divine destiny.   This powerful, practical man shows you how to tap into power you did not even know you had. – Brian Tracy – Author, *The Power of Self Confidence*

I found myself savoring the concepts of the Law of Attraction merging with the Law of Creativity until slowly the beautiful truths seeped deeper into my thirsty soul.   I am called to be a Creator!   My friend, Dr. Jeremy Lopez, has a way of reminding us of our eternal 'I-Am-ness' while putting the tools in our hands to unlock our endless creative

the platform with him at a number of conferences. Through this time, I have found him as a man of integrity, commitment, wisdom, and one of the most networked people I have met. Jeremy is an entrepreneur and a leader of leaders. He has amazing insights into leadership competencies and values. He has a passion to ignite this latent potential within individuals and organizations and provide ongoing development and coaching to bring about competitive advantage and success. I would highly recommend him as a speaker, coach, mentor, and consultant. – Chris Gaborit – Learning Leader, Trainer

DEDICATION

I dare you to believe in the abundant life again.   I dare you to begin to reach for your dreams again and bring to life all of those visions of yesteryear that you allowed to fall by the wayside of life. My prayer for you, both now and always, is that you would begin to realize just how deserving you truly are of the life you keep dreaming of.

CONTENTS

Introduction   p.1

Section One   p.7

Section Two   p.27

Section Three   p.45

INTRODUCTION

I believe in success, because I believe in God. It's defined me for as long as I can remember and has been a driving force in the work and ministry of Identity Network for more than thirty years. I love seeing people empowered. Nothing gives me greater joy than to see men and women, just like you, awaken to their fullest potential in God and to live out the abundance they were destined to receive.

In my newest book, Universal Laws: Are They Biblical? I ask a very important, somewhat existential question: Can success be guaranteed one-hundred percent of the time? Is there a way to ensure that we never fail?   Although there will always be moments of setback and heartache and although in this world we will have moments of tribulation, just like Jesus promised, is it possible to actually guarantee success through it all? Is there some secret to actually getting what we want in life?

It seems like such a simple question, at first glance.   However, to truly ponder the topic means to delve even more deeply than ever before into the mechanics of the Laws at work within Creation.   Throughout the years, I've shared many of the principles of the Laws of Creation; however, this is the first time I've ever shared the teachings in sch a practical way.   There are Laws that govern all of Creation - Laws that, when adhered to, will always guarantee specific outcomes.   We know this.

But what does that really look like in practicality? What does a life lived according to those Laws really resemble?

In my newest book, "Universal Laws: Are They Biblical? I share universal Laws in a much more practical, more personal way. Is the Law of Attraction Biblical? Yes! Jesus referred to it a lot, actually. He simply called it "faith." Jesus spoke of belief more than any other topic, and belief and thought are the catalysts of attraction and creation. But what does that look like in daily life? How does that help to land the new job and more rewarding career or bring in and attract the new relationship? Are there ways to actually guarantee success in all areas of life? Yes. Within the book, I share also the power of the Law of Vibration - a Law that so often goes unnoticed.

"Your vibe attracts." This principle in life is the foundation for all manifestation and for all prophetic alignment. Within the prophetic movement, there is often so much talk of "alignment" – alignment to the will and the plan of God. What we often fail to recognize, though, is the significance of our own alignment within our own selves - spirit, soul, and body. The one and only reason you have yet to attract the life you truly want and desire is not because of some attack of the enemy or some devil, and it isn't because of a lack of alignment with God. The reason is because of a lack of alignment within your own self, within the realm of your own thoughts, emotions, and desires.

When we begin to put away limited thinking and begin to think of life in a much more expansive way than ever before, we become more aligned and more "in tune" with the energy of Creation, aligning to our desired and intended outcomes. If something feels out of alignment for you, it's because it is. It is time to examine it. It is time to go within and to delve into the motives, the thoughts, and the intentions within your own self. After all, that is where the Kingdom of Heaven truly lies.

SECTION ONE
DESIRE

If you truly desire more, you are going to have to raise your awareness and your belief to match the "more" you claim to desire. You are going to have to vibe higher! Part of why you may feel that your current job or current relationship is literally "draining" the life out of you is because you have outgrown them. That is not some cliche or analogy of spiritual enlightenment; it is actually quite literal. If you feel this way, the spiritual, energetic reason is that the past holds a vibration that does not match the vibration of your future. Feelings matter, and it is important to become more discerning with all of the feelings of life.

While writing the book, I began to feel even more of a sense of inspiration to share the power of thoughts as they relate to the overall desires we have in life. Yes; contrary to popular belief and despite what religion may seek to claim, your desires actually do matter. In fact, your desires have been implanted within you by God and possess the keys to your very own destiny in God.

What if I were to tell you that there's a reason you have the desire you have? That its not mere wishful thinking or the result of some overactive imagination but that it's, in fact, the very fuel that will propel you forward into the life you keep dreaming of? As you read my newest book, Universal Laws: Are They Biblical? What you're going to begin to see and realize more and more is that you've been given a role to play in the "game" of life and that life has never been merely a spectator sport.

And when they came nigh to Jerusalem, unto Bethphage and Bethany, at the mount of Olives, he sendeth forth two of his disciples,

2 And saith unto them, Go your way into the village over against you: and as soon as ye be entered into it, ye shall find a colt tied, whereon never man sat; loose him, and bring him.

3 And if any man say unto you, Why do ye this? say ye that the Lord hath need of him; and straightway he will send him hither.

4 And they went their way, and found the colt tied by the door without in a place where two ways met; and they loose him.

5 And certain of them that stood there said unto them, What do ye, loosing the colt?

6 And they said unto them even as Jesus had commanded: and they let them go.

7 And they brought the colt to Jesus, and cast their garments on him; and he sat upon him.

8 And many spread their garments in the way: and others cut down branches off the trees, and strawed them in the way.

9 And they that went before, and they that followed, cried, saying, Hosanna; Blessed is he that cometh in the name of the Lord:

10 Blessed be the kingdom of our father David, that cometh in the name of the Lord: Hosanna in the highest.

11 And Jesus entered into Jerusalem, and into the temple: and when he had looked round about upon all things, and now the eventide was come, he went out unto Bethany with the twelve.

12 And on the morrow, when they were come from Bethany, he was hungry:

13 And seeing a fig tree afar off having leaves, he came, if haply he might find any thing thereon: and when he came to

it, he found nothing but leaves; for the time of figs was not yet.

14 And Jesus answered and said unto it, No man eat fruit of thee hereafter for ever. And his disciples heard it.

15 And they come to Jerusalem: and Jesus went into the temple, and began to cast out them that sold and bought in the temple, and overthrew the tables of the moneychangers, and the seats of them that sold doves;

16 And would not suffer that any man should carry any vessel through the temple.

17 And he taught, saying unto them, Is it not written, My house shall be called of

all nations the house of prayer? but ye have made it a den of thieves.

18 And the scribes and chief priests heard it, and sought how they might destroy him: for they feared him, because all the people was astonished at his doctrine.

19 And when even was come, he went out of the city.

20 And in the morning, as they passed by, they saw the fig tree dried up from the roots.

21 And Peter calling to remembrance saith unto him, Master, behold, the fig tree which thou cursedst is withered away.

22 And Jesus answering saith unto them, Have faith in God.

23 For verily I say unto you, That whosoever shall say unto this mountain, Be thou removed, and be thou cast into the sea; and shall not doubt in his heart, but shall believe that those things which he saith shall come to pass; he shall have whatsoever he saith.

24 Therefore I say unto you, What things soever ye desire, when ye pray, believe that ye receive them, and ye shall have them.

25 And when ye stand praying, forgive, if ye have ought against any: that your Father also which is in heaven may forgive you your trespasses.

26 But if ye do not forgive, neither will your Father which is in heaven forgive your trespasses.

27 And they come again to Jerusalem: and as he was walking in the temple, there come to him the chief priests, and the scribes, and the elders,

28 And say unto him, By what authority doest thou these things? and who gave thee this authority to do these things?

29 And Jesus answered and said unto them, I will also ask of you one question, and answer me, and I will tell you by what authority I do these things.

30 The baptism of John, was it from heaven, or of men? answer me.

31 And they reasoned with themselves, saying, If we shall say, From heaven; he will say, Why then did ye not believe him?

32 But if we shall say, Of men; they feared the people: for all men counted John, that he was a prophet indeed.

33 And they answered and said unto Jesus, We cannot tell. And Jesus answering saith unto them, Neither do I tell you by what authority I do these things. (Mark 11:1-33 KJV)

It's one of the most quoted, most studied and most revered passages of text within the scriptures - Jesus speaking of the power of belief. According to Jesus, if we believe and doubt not, we'll be given exactly what we believe. What's so often overlooked or casually dismissed within the passage, though, is the 24th verse of text. "Therefore I say unto you, What things soever ye desire, when ye pray, believe that ye receive them, and ye shall have them."

"Desire." It seems like such a simple concept, doesn't it? It seems like nothing more than "want." However, "desire" is not simply "want," as you will see when reading my newest book. Desire is much, much more a driving, inner force and is, in many ways, the actual fuel of Creation itself. Even the psalmist seemed to know the power of desire at work within Creation:
Fret not thyself because of evildoers, neither be thou envious against the workers of iniquity.

2 For they shall soon be cut down like the grass, and wither as the green herb.

3 Trust in the Lord, and do good; so shalt thou dwell in the land, and verily thou shalt be fed.

4 Delight thyself also in the Lord: and he shall give thee the desires of thine heart.

5 Commit thy way unto the Lord; trust also in him; and he shall bring it to pass.

6 And he shall bring forth thy righteousness as the light, and thy judgment as the noonday.

7 Rest in the Lord, and wait patiently for him: fret not thyself because of him who prospereth in his way, because of the

man who bringeth wicked devices to pass. (Psalm 37:1-7 KJV)

What I've found throughout years of success coaching and leadership training is that most individuals never truly achieve their dreams and manifest their goals because they never allow themselves to have a clear picture of what it is they truly desire. If, according to the scriptures, we're given the desires of our hearts, don't you think it's high time that you begin to finally answer the question once and for all, "What do I really desire?" When you begin to become aligned with your desire and with your vision for your own life and destiny, there is absolutely nothing that will be able to stop you from taking action.

I want you to take a moment and cast vision for your own life.   Right now, the Universe and all of Heaven and earth are asking you a very real, very powerful question: "What do you truly desire?" In the space provided, I want you to describe, in detail, at least five desires that you feel destined to have.   What are the things you'd like to accomplish? Be descriptive.

____

____

____

____

____

____

____

SECTION TWO
RAISING VIBRATION

Chapter Three within my newest book, Universal Laws: Are They Biblical? Is entitled "Vibes."   In truth, it was one of my personal favorite chapters to write within the book.   As you'll see when reading the book, all of Creation - and, indeed, all of life - is constantly moving. If we aren't careful, we'll be left behind and feel lost in the current of the ocean if we don't make the decision to move and to flow with life.   But has it ever felt as though you're always paddling upstream, against the current?   Has it sometimes felt as though no matter what you do, you just can't seem to get ahead?   Let me ask it another way. Has it ever felt like the current of life was working against you rather than working for you? If you answered "yes," the reason isn't because you're under attack - although it may sometimes feel that way. The reason is simply because you're out of alignment within your thoughts and your own perspective. When I wrote the bestselling book Creating with Your Thoughts years ago, I wanted to share the power of the Kingdom Law of Attraction in a new and revelatory way. For decades now, much has been said about and written about the The Universal Law of Attraction. It's been the topic of quite a few international bestsellers and more than a few hit movies. "The Secret," to this day, is one of the most popular books ever written, and it isn't really all that hard to see and understand why.   Everyone wants more.   Everyone wants a better, more fulfilling life.   We all have dreams and desires for a better, more rewarding future.   Jesus knew this, and promised an abundant life - a life where there's nothing missing, nothing lacking, and nothing broken.   Jesus actually had a lot to share about the Universal Law of Attraction.   He called it, simply, "faith." With faith, he said, all things are possible - especially for them that believe.

What if I were to tell you, though, that faith and belief aren't merely some thoughts forms or ideas floating around in space?   What if I told you that your beliefs actually hold real, physical, tangible power?   Belief isn't like some fairy dust, and it isn't just wishful thinking.   For that matter, it isn't even hoping.   It's more than that.

There actually is a very real power and a very real "force" at work behind faith. When Jesus spoke of the power to move mountains with our faith, there was a reason for it.   The reason is because faith is a force that's actually always moving.

And after six days Jesus taketh Peter, James, and John his brother, and bringeth them up into an high mountain apart,

2 And was transfigured before them: and his face did shine as the sun, and his raiment was white as the light.

3 And, behold, there appeared unto them Moses and Elias talking with him.

4 Then answered Peter, and said unto Jesus, Lord, it is good for us to be here: if thou wilt, let us make here three tabernacles; one for thee, and one for Moses, and one for Elias.

5 While he yet spake, behold, a bright cloud overshadowed them: and behold a voice out of the cloud, which said, This is my beloved Son, in whom I am well pleased; hear ye him.

6 And when the disciples heard it, they fell on their face, and were sore afraid.

7 And Jesus came and touched them, and said, Arise, and be not afraid.

8 And when they had lifted up their eyes, they saw no man, save Jesus only.

9 And as they came down from the mountain, Jesus charged them, saying, Tell the vision to no man, until the Son of man be risen again from the dead.

10 And his disciples asked him, saying, Why then say the scribes that Elias must first come?

11 And Jesus answered and said unto them, Elias truly shall first come, and restore all things.

12 But I say unto you, That Elias is come already, and they knew him not, but have done unto him whatsoever they listed. Likewise shall also the Son of man suffer of them.

13 Then the disciples understood that he spake unto them of John the Baptist.

14 And when they were come to the multitude, there came to him a certain man, kneeling down to him, and saying,

15 Lord, have mercy on my son: for he is lunatick, and sore vexed: for ofttimes he falleth into the fire, and oft into the water.

16 And I brought him to thy disciples, and they could not cure him.

17 Then Jesus answered and said, O faithless and perverse generation, how long shall I be with you? how long shall I suffer you? bring him hither to me.

18 And Jesus rebuked the devil; and he departed out of him: and the child was cured from that very hour.

19 Then came the disciples to Jesus apart, and said, Why could not we cast him out?

20 And Jesus said unto them, Because of your unbelief: for verily I say unto you, If ye have faith as a grain of mustard seed, ye shall say unto this mountain, Remove hence to yonder place; and it shall remove; and nothing shall be impossible unto you. (Matthew 17:1-20 KJV)

There's a reason faith can move mountains. It's because our thoughts and our beliefs actually have very real movement - a very real vibration! When we talk about the Law of Attraction or even the Law of Creation, for that matter, there's actually another Universal Law at work behind both.

The Law at work is actually the Law of Vibration

According to the site "The Joy Within," "If you've heard of The Law of Attraction, you've probably heard the phrase: your thoughts create your reality.

This idea has been around for centuries, but it's often misunderstood, and many people don't understand why or how The Law of Attraction works.

The key is to recognize that The Law of Attraction is actually based on a more fundamental Law of Vibration, which states that everything you experience is nothing more than a vibration.
On the surface, knowing that everything is a vibration can be somewhat confusing, so in this post I'm going to

break it down and explain The Law of Vibration through 3 easy concepts.

Ready?

What Is The Law of Vibration and How Does It Work?

As I mentioned above, The Law of Vibration is simply the idea that everything exists, fundamentally, as vibration. This concept is firmly supported by quantum physics.

Practically speaking, you can break it down into three core understandings:

Everything is energy.

Your thoughts, beliefs, and emotions create your vibration.

When you change your vibration, everything changes.

Everything Is Energy

Firstly, it's essential that you understand that everything in the physical world is nothing more than energy. This is what Einstein proved to us with his infamous formula, $E = mc^2$. This means that physically speaking, there is no difference between matter and energy, since each is simply one form of the other.

To grasp this, think of the analogy of ice, water, and steam. Each is the same thing. It's all water, even though each has its own set of unique properties, and you can easily change the state of water by changing the temperature of it. Vibration works in much the same way.

You might also know that on a quantum level, physical matter is not nearly as dense as we think it is. The distance between electrons in an atom is comparable to the distance between stars in a galaxy. There is a vast amount of nothingness within what we think is "solid."

Not only that, but those electrons are constantly changing state, popping into and out of a state of "matter" and a state of "pure energy" all of the time. Quite literally, everything is energy.

This means that you, too, are only energy, and the same rules that apply to the chair you're sitting in, apply to your own body and brain. This leads us to our next point.

Your Thoughts, Beliefs, and Emotions Create Your Vibration

If you are energy, then what creates your individual vibration?

While your aggregate vibration is influenced by a number of different factors, the most important elements to consider are your thoughts, your beliefs, and your emotions.

How you think, what you believe, and how you feel are the three most important indicators that tell you what your vibration is. They're also the three points you can consciously use to develop control over your vibration.

To put it simply: the better you feel, the higher your individual energy, and the faster your vibration. This means when you focus on feeling good, what you're really doing is changing your vibration to a higher state of energy.

This is the crux of empowerment. You can learn to train yourself to be happy, all of the time, so that your vibration attracts positive experiences to you. Check out these easy happiness hacks to get started.

When You Change Your Vibration, Everything Changes

If you and everything around you exists in a state of vibration, it follows logically that as you move through your day-to-day life, you don't actually experience an objective physical world. You experience a vibrational aggregate, which only exists at that one, very specific level of vibration.

If you change your vibration, everything you experience will change. Most of the time, we don't notice this change because we stay within the same range of vibration, oscillating back and forth between good and bad moods, all while remaining mostly stagnant.

If, however, you determine to take control of your thoughts, beliefs, and emotions, you can change your vibration instantly, and begin to experience a new world.

Chances are, this idea will sound fanciful, until you begin to experience it for yourself. Notice the synchronicity in the world around you, and what how your experiences correlate to your thoughts, beliefs, and emotions.

Observing your role in this way is the beginning of conscious manifestation."

.Desire is key within the Kingdom of God.   And, believe it or not, it's actually more practical than religion would ever dare to publicly admit. What if we could realize that we actually aren't at war with the Creator and that our wants and desires aren't somehow separating us from God?   What if it were true that our desires actually are the desires of God?   Can you even imagine the weight that would be removed if we could begin to view life from this perspective?   The possibilities would be endless!   Could it be that all things truly are possible for them that believe?

As the Scriptures remind us, just as He is, so are we in this present world.

The universal Laws remind us of the importance of being in alignment with the things we desire.   They remind us of the power of personal choice and also of personal responsibility.

When you align yourself with your truest, deepest desires and then, within your thoughts and beliefs, align yourself to those desires, absolutely nothing will be able to stop you!   As I share within the book, though, there actually a very real reason for this.   The reason is because, once you know what you want, you'll do whatever it takes to get what you want. You don't have to fight against the current of life, always feeling tossed about and thrown about by the waves of change.   When you realize that you are the one controlling the experiences of your life according to your own thoughts, your own beliefs, and your own perspective, all of the sudden life will stop seeming so unexpected and so uncertain. It's easy to predict the future when you realize that you've always had a say in writing that future. As a co-creator with God, you have every right to write the future you actually want and desire.

SECTION THREE
OVERCOMING
OBSTACLES

The abundant life that Jesus promised is already yours, and it's time you realize it. All of those dreams and visions you keep having, imagining and longing for a better, brighter future, are proof-positive that the life of your dreams is already yours for the taking. When writing the book, I wanted to offer words of inspiration, also, to remind you just how close you truly are from achieving all that you desire.

The truth of the matter is that you're actually closer than it may seem.   The new career isn't really that far away. The new relationship is just one meeting away. The financial freedom are just a few decisions away, and a life that feels better is just a single thought away. As you journey through the pages of my newest book, Universal Laws: Are They Biblical? I want you to feel, first, a sense of optimism and hope again. Yes; those feelings matter. And you have every right to live a life that feels good. In chapters three and four, I share insight into the importance of connecting to desire. What does desire look like in practicality? How do we know if we truly want something?

What I've realized, though, within my own life and throughout countless millions of prophetic readings over more than twenty-five years is that the single greatest obstacle to achieving our goals is not simply a lack of belief in the goal or a lack of faith.   The greatest obstacle comes in the form of all of those inner conversations where we doubt our own worth.   Hear me when I say that in spite of all your faith and all your belief, absolutely nothing will hinder you from harnessing the Universal Laws to work for you quite like self-doubt and a feeling of unworthiness.   It's all too common, really.   "Jeremy, no one will ever love me after the things I've done."   "I'll never be able to start my own business because I have nothing to offer."   "I'll never be out of debt because I don't make enough to even pay the bills I already have."   And on and on it goes, really.

The greatest obstacle to your manifestation of, well, anything you want is your own self-talk - within your own thoughts about yourself. You see, prophetically speaking, it's not enough to simply have a clear vision for the future, and it's really not even enough to have a desire for the future. Somewhere along the way, if you're ever going to truly manifest the dream life you want, you're going to have to begin to actually see yourself in that future, so that you can align with it and take the necessary steps needed to get there. It's time to not only imagine and dream of the new career; it's time to also see yourself in it - worthy of it and thriving. It's time to see yourself in the new relationship already, feeling love and giving love. I closed my newest book, Universal Laws: Are They Biblical? With a chapter entitled "The God Life." It's really more than just a catchy title to a chapter, really. It's the greatest principle within the Universal Laws.

"You are not separate from God." Read that again. The life that you now live is the life of God Himself in the realm of earth! As the scriptures remind us over and over again, just as He is, so are we. That isn't some religious hyperbole or cliche. It's the truth of the Universal Laws. You are a powerful, thinking, speaking spirit, possessing all the power of the Godhead bodily. Just as He is, so are you. And so it's time begin to actually see not only your dreams and desires in a different way than ever before, but it's time to also see yourself differently too! It's time to realize just how deserving you are. That begins by tackling the limiting beliefs that have held you back for so long.

(In the following exercise, I want you to think of the goals you hope to manifest. In this exercise, we're going to tackle the limitations in your feelings that are keeping you from connecting to the life you deserve)

Do you have the experience needed for the career you truly desire?   If not, what steps are you taking to gain that experience?

What part of yourself, physically, do you feel most insecure about as far as your appearance?   How has this affected the way you interact with other people?

If you're currently single and search of a new relationship, what frightens you the most about meeting new people?   Do you feel a fear of rejection in those first, initial meetings?   If so, why?

Has there been a history of financial lack within your family, with everyone always struggling to find and to make money?   What was this like, growing up?   Would you say that your parents did the best they could have done with what they had?   What choices are you capable of making differently, now going forward?

These seem such simple questions, don't they?   They seem so surface-level, at first glance.   However, the way you answer those questions will say a lot about your own process and your very own self-limiting beliefs.   These are questions I pose in coaching sessions with clients throughout the world.   You see, at the end of the day, every change - whether for the good or for the not so good - comes from the way in which we view our own selves. Your process of manifestations isn't independent of you; it's a process taking place through you - as you. The sooner you're able to see and recognize the role that you're playing within the creation of your very own life, the sooner you'll begin to see that you have the power to change the course of your life, by shifting your perspective.

We all dream of the "good" life." None are exempted from this. There's something within humanity that causes us to want to always attain more and to reach for higher, more lofty dreams. The good life, though, is actually the "God" life. All good things come from above, from Him. You, my friend and fellow seeker, are just as much a Creator as He is, and just as He is, so are you in this present world.   If you're not experiencing the good life, you have no one to blame.   The choices you make are entirely your very own.

I've included as part of this comprehensive study guide a section designed to be your own personal journal.   As you journey through the pages of my newest book, you'll receive insight into how you can change your own life by changing your thinking.   I invite you to use the journal section within the book and workbook to take notes, write down feelings, and your own prayers and dreams.   The more you learn to connect with those deeper feelings and those deeper, more hidden thoughts, the sooner you'll uncover the

greatest truth of all.   You are the
Creator!

ABOUT THE AUTHOR

Dr. Jeremy Lopez is Founder and President of Identity Network and Now Is Your Moment. Identity Network is one of the world's leading prophetic resource sites, offering books, teachings, and courses to a global audience. For more than thirty years, Dr. Lopez has been considered a pioneering voice within the field of the prophetic arts and his proven strategies for success coaching are now being implemented by various training groups and faith groups throughout the world. Dr. Lopez is the author of more than forty books, including his international bestselling books The Universe is at Your Command and Creating with Your Thoughts. Throughout his career, he has spoken prophetically into the lives of heads of business as well as heads of state. He has ministered to Governor Bob Riley of the State of Alabama, Prime Minister Benjamin Netanyahu, and Shimon Peres. Dr. Lopez continues to be a highly sought conference teacher and host, speaking on the topics of human potential and spirituality.

ADDITIONAL WORKS

Prophetic Transformation

The Universe is at Your Command: Vibrating the Creative Side of God

Creating with Your Thoughts

Creating Your Soul Map: Manifesting the Future You with a Vision Board

Creating Your Soul Map: A Visionary Workbook

Abandoned to Divine Destiny

The Law of Attraction: Universal Power of Spirit

PROPHETIC READINGS

What does the future hold for you? What dreams, visions and promises await you? You have been promised an abundant life, and prophetic promises are yours to claim. Considered a pioneering voice within the prophetic movement, Dr. Jeremy Lopez shares prophetic insight with millions throughout the world. Schedule your very own prophetic reading with Dr. Lopez by contacting the office of Identity Network.

JOURNAL